Setting up a Family Office

Authors
Keith Drewery and Barbara R Hauser

Managing director
Sian O'Neill

Setting up a Family Office
is published by

Globe Law and Business Ltd
3 Mylor Close
Horsell
Woking
Surrey GU21 4DD
United Kingdom
Tel: +44 20 3745 4770
www.globelawandbusiness.com

Printed and bound in Great Britain by Ashford Colour Press Ltd

Setting up a Family Office

ISBN 9781787423183
EPUB ISBN 9781787423190
Adobe PDF ISBN 9781787423206
Mobi ISBN 9781787423213

Table of contents

I. Introduction

Family offices seem to increase in number on a continual – and a global – basis. What are they and why are they increasingly popular? What sort of family is a good candidate for a family office? For a family who are interested in creating their own family office, where do they begin?

Families with significant capital resources have long used defined processes and systems to organise their financial affairs for maximum utility, security and peace of mind, driven principally by a desire to preserve and perpetuate the benefits of wealth for future generations. More recently, the central role and purpose of the family office has evolved to provide a distinct set of services designed around the wider needs and objectives of the family.

We offer this Special Report as a practical guide on how to decide whether your family would benefit from having a family office and, if so, to explain how to go about its creation, operation and expansion.[1]

1. What is a family office?

First, some background. Where did the term 'family office' come from? Arguably, it is not a new concept but a new label, originating during the era of the industrial barons in the United States – the Rockefellers, Bessemers, Morgans, Pitcairns – all of whom had family offices. Of course, the concept of staff dedicated to the needs of a family has been around a great deal longer than that. Only the name has changed. In medieval England the steward oversaw the household staff and managed the family's wealth, including the land.[2] In Japan, the *monban* or 'gatekeeper' guarded the privacy of the family.

So, what is a family office today? There is a saying in the family office industry: "If you've seen one family office ... you've seen one family office." The point, of course, is how different the offices can be. Barbara Hauser, in her seminal article on family offices in 2001,[3] wrote that the definition of a family office was vague enough to cover everything from a one-person, part-time assistant to a full-service private trust company with a staff of dozens.[4] Indeed, we know a family office in the United States that consists of one person – a family member – and his administrative assistant. He calls himself a family office and is quite active in the industry. At the other end we know an office in Geneva with more than sixty staff for one couple and their two young children – with a full-time art curator based in London.

Simply put, a family office consists of one or more staff members dedicated to the needs of a family. It is a family's tactical response to the strategic decision to safeguard the financial rewards of their hard work for future generations or the community at large. Those needs vary considerably over time and from family to family. There may be one employee or more than a hundred. Elsewhere, a family office has been defined as "a private company of dedicated professionals devoted exclusively to the investment, personal and legacy needs of one family".[5]

Our focus in this report will be on the traditional single family office (SFO), and not on the bewildering array of self-styled 'multi-family' offices (MFOs), often used to attract wealthy clients.

Most family offices do manage the family's wealth and investment portfolios. This is not always the case. For example, there is a trend in the United States to treat the investment management role as a service that can be outsourced, as many families now consider investment management to be more of a commodity than an individually skilled area. In the case of a family office that is exclusively dedicated to the investment function, we think the more accurate label is 'private investment firm'.

In our experience the most valuable service a new family office staff can provide is to make a comprehensive, consolidated inventory of all of the assets owned by the family. The inventory can then be appraised, the cash needs of the family matched to the income produced, and so on.

"Simply put, a family office consists of one or more staff members dedicated to the needs of a family. It is a family's tactical response to the strategic decision to safeguard the financial rewards of their hard work for future generations or the community at large."

We find that very few wealthy families have the benefit of consolidated statements enabling them to evaluate performances and diversification. Instead, wealth is often accumulated on an ad hoc, even haphazard basis. We have both spent time helping families understand what they own. This is an essential step.

2. The increasing popularity of the family office
One estimate is that there at 12–15,000 family offices globally.[6] Of these, it is thought is that more than 6,000 are in the United States. The numbers are impossible to verify since by their nature these offices value privacy and in general have no reporting requirements – we are certainly aware of a number of truly private family offices.

We think the apparent increase is due to several factors:

- a decrease in the number of trusted global financial institutions;
- the increasing number of very wealthy families;
- an increase in local aggressiveness in reporting and taxing;
- the complexity of family holdings;
- a number of well-publicised investment frauds; and
- consideration of the future needs of the family, including how to train the next generation to manage the family wealth.

An additional factor is the success of a founding entrepreneur, who may feel skilled enough to take over the family's investment management. The increase in common fund offerings by institutions and the inevitable preference for such products encourage the entrepreneur to take over the investment management role. By forming a new SFO, the entrepreneur is assured loyalty and the absence of any conflict of interest. On the other hand, some entrepreneurs who were successful managing an operating business feel at a loss when the business is sold and they have investment assets to manage. It is a world and a skillset that can seem daunting, and this may be a logical time to form an SFO.

II. How to use this Special Report

This Special Report is written with the main objective that it should be accessible and practical. To more informed eyes it may seem rather simplistic but hopefully our remarks, if made from a less than academic perspective, will be seen as appropriate and on point.

Fundamentally, this is a guide for those who may be aware of the existence of family offices but to whom they remain a mystery. The report breaks down into a logical sequence what you may want to contemplate if you, your family or the clients you work for have been fortunate enough to achieve a level of financial success beyond that which may be consumed to satisfy a pleasant retirement.

The chapters and sections are divided into the steps through which we would typically walk a family in their discussions around the two questions, "What do we do now?" and "How do we make sure that we are in a position to take advantage of the benefits we have received, over the long term?".

In the next chapter, "Should I have a family office?" there is a table with a list of the most relevant questions to consider, including perhaps the most important: "Do I actually need to set up a family office?" Whether you do or you don't, being able to explore the answer to the first two questions in the table will at least give you a head start in thinking about what may be an alternative – and hopefully better – way to manage your family's financial affairs.

Some people come later to the idea of setting up a family office, having spent years concentrating on their business and its success. Being aware of the time in your life and what is going on in the lives of your children and possibly your grandchildren offers a wonderful perspective on getting the set-up right from the start. It is not just about setting up a family office; it is also about understanding what you and your family have together, as a unit.

The report offers practical and implementable ideas but it is important that you invest time in understanding your own motivations, and those of your family, by exploring the ideas and questions posed in the pages that follow.

We suggest that you try to keep your initial discussions with other family members as broad as possible. It is, after all, expected to be an office for the whole family. The extent of the wider family's involvement, however, will to some extent depend on the circumstances. It may be that you have enjoyed early success in a business endeavour, in which case your children may be too young to ask their opinion. Or perhaps you are a second or later generation family member interested to learn which of your siblings and cousins may be interested in the idea of a family office – in this scenario you may well be leading your family in a discussion over which you have relatively little control.

We have sought to order the chapters of this report in such a way as to provide a logical framework for decision making. Chapters III and IV deal with questions of substance: Why have an office at all? What kind will be most suitable? Later chapters deal with design issues such as what the family office will do, where it should it be located and how it will be funded.

By way of conclusion, we offer a view as to what the life cycle of a family office may look like in the future. It may be organised as a private company but this does not mean that it will run itself. It will require demonstrable leadership and clear communication between the family and the office personnel to ensure that it remains relevant to the family.

We hope you find this report useful and would be delighted to hear how you, your family and your advisers have approached the possibility of setting up your own family office. Our email addresses are in the biographical notes at the back of the report.

III. Should I have a family office?

As the concept of the family office has gained currency, individuals considering how best to manage their wealth have been asking with increasing frequency, "Should we have one?".

It is an important question to ask before committing time, energy and resources to the establishment of what may prove to be something that doesn't meet the family's needs.

Recognising the symptoms
International accounting firm Armanino has five simple statements against which to assess whether it might be time to consider a family office:[7]

1. ***Too many go-to advisers:*** *You receive countless emails, phone calls and communications from your trusted legal, financial and investment advisers. You're starting to become overwhelmed.*

2. ***Financial chaos:*** *You have numerous bills, file folders, stacks of paper, jammed office drawers and multiple household employees. It's becoming a real struggle to keep track of everything. You need help with your tax payments and filings, insurance renewals and coverage assessments, capital calls and commitments and collectibles management.*

3. ***Professional vs personal:*** *You trust your employees and you allow them to help manage portions of your personal life, giving them access to your finances and personal net worth, but haven't done anything to protect yourself against unauthorised use of this access.*

4. ***Trustworthy decisions:*** *You have a number of trusts created to protect your wealth, but you're unsure if your trustees are aware of the responsibilities and requirements needed to fulfil their fiduciary duties.*

5. ***Family education:*** *As your family matures, you want your spouse and the next generation to become actively involved in learning how you manage your wealth, but you're not sure where to begin.*

If you recognise any of these 'symptoms' you may want to assess the benefit of a family office as the cure.

1. Structure

Before embarking on an exercise to see whether it is worth setting up a family office, we need to understand what a family office is or, equally important, what it is not. It does not have a defined legal structure, legal identity or specific traits or characteristics that provide some extraordinary benefits or unique opportunities.

Unlike a corporate entity, which offers limited liability and asset protection for shareholders, or a family trust, which provides trustees with a defined set of rules – in a trust deed – to detail how they should deal with property on behalf of beneficiaries, the family office does not have a prescribed form.

Instead, the structure of the family office is for the family themselves to define, based on what they want their wealth to be used for.

2. Key questions

It is helpful to start by asking a few key questions.

2.1 What does being wealthy mean to me and my family?

For many wealthy families there is a clear understanding of what constitutes their wealth – a particular commercial property, for example, is owned by XYZ Limited, the family's investment vehicle.

What may be less well defined or understood is why. To what end do we possess wealth? Being quite clear as to what being wealthy offers to you and your family helps to define how you might think about the management of your wealth, and the possible role of a family office.

If you see the purpose of wealth as being its preservation for the benefit of your children, their children and future generations, the mechanism you need to put in place to help realise this ambition will be key.

2.2 What aspirations do I have for my children?
We all want the best for our children regardless of financial resources available to the family. However, it is reasonable to be concerned as to the impact upon them of having access to money and wealth.

How you see that wealth benefitting your children and grandchildren will go a long way to determining whether an SFO is what you need and, if so, what exactly it will do.

2.3 What legacy would I like to leave behind?
One of the benefits of financial success, particularly if you've been responsible for it, is the ability to define your own legacy and use your wealth to help do so.

That may be in the form of philanthropy – the funding of hospitals and universities, for example – or making provision for what the family does in the future and to what extent its activities are inspired by your story.

Whatever you define as your legacy, there may be a need to ensure that it is preserved and protected.

2.4 How close would I like my family to be in 20 years' time?
This question is a good one because it focuses on the future of the key element of a family office – the family themselves. Wealth doesn't determine whether your children's children get along as cousins but it does at least help the family to come together around a sense of shared ownership. In the absence of other forums, the family office can give impetus to the idea that the family should remain close across generations, and provide the practical means by which that is achieved.

If, by an examination of these questions, you become convinced of the benefit of the family being engaged across generations as the joint owners of the family capital, it is very likely that you will see the need to create a family office.

In conclusion, therefore, a need for a family office becomes most profound when:

- the family get older without there being a formal succession process;

- the family want to remain close as joint owners of capital;
- the family appreciate the need to be educated about the management of their wealth;
- the family are unlikely to have a second 'liquidation event' necessitating the careful management of existing resources; and
- the family's affairs are complex and would benefit from being coordinated across professional service providers.

By way of recap, you might like to consider the following table in assessing your own family's needs and objectives.

Table 1. Needs and objectives

Step	Initial consideration	Objective	Outcome
Define the family's goals and objectives	What does the family want to do and why does it want to do it?	Gain consensus as to the benefits of being a family whose affairs are managed collectively	Provide the basis for decision making
Assess current position	What is the current position?	Articulate how service is currently delivered to the family	Define what works and doesn't work, what fits and doesn't fit
Outline the needs of the family	What services does the family need?	Summarise the role that would be played by a family office	Highlight service requirements
Define a new structure	How are the service needs of the family met?	Begin designing the structure of a family office	Enable a broad business plan to be put together
Set goals and objectives for the family office	How is the 'performance' of the family office measured?	Define the family's expectations as regards overall costs of delivery and revenue performance	Develop a coherent strategy by defining the capacity of the family office to deliver services
Communicate strategy to stakeholders	How is the transition from the current view to the better view to be managed?	Develop a plan for implementation	Set timeframes and allocate responsibility for moving to a new regime

3. Alternatives to an SFO

This is important, as it may be that the most appropriate structure to help manage your family's affairs is not an SFO but one of the alternatives listed below. Depending on what you'd like the family office itself to do, and what you would like to outsource, it may be an option to work collaboratively using one or more of these various options.

3.1 Join a multi-family office

MFOs come in several varieties. The most common is one that began as an SFO, then expanded by adding new clients. Less common is one created at the outset by more than one family. And finally, there is the MFO that is more like a marketing brand. You will want to consider the pros and cons of each, but taken together they are as follows:

Pros: The services and staff are already in place and the office is in full operation. The costs are known.

Cons: Loyalty is shared by the other families; it is not exclusive to your family. There may be conflicts of interest among the various families. Privacy is not so guaranteed.

3.2 Become a client of an institution's family office practice

You will discover that many of the major financial firms offer services under the heading of Family Offices. Even accounting firms and some law firms hold themselves out as providing family office services.

Pros: It is fairly easy to become a client of a large institution's family office division.

Cons: It is often true that the institution is partly motivated by the fees it can charge for investment management. Other services may be downplayed as they function as a cost centre. Also, it is not universal practice to offer truly independent advice; the firm's own investment products are often favoured.

3.3 Form a virtual family office

Another idea is to forego a separate building to house the family office, and instead to organise the existing professionals into one virtual family office.[8]

Pros: Existing advisers are used – with no additional cost. No funds need to be used to furnish a physical office.

Cons: It is difficult to coordinate all of the advisers. Indeed, this is one of the primary benefits, in our opinion, of having your own dedicated bricks and mortar office.

3.4 Form a 'hybrid'

This model, promoted by Barbara Hauser in her early writings, remains a sound proposition today. The idea is to have a very small number of full-time family office staff.

Pros: A small group interacts closely with the family, understands their needs and outsources as necessary.

Cons: A small group may be overwhelmed by the number and variety of duties, eventually wishing to hire additional staff.

3.5 Partner with a multi-family office

In this model, you retain your own identity as a family office to interface with the family, and give the administration and investment management function to a third-party multi-family office.

Pros: The back office of a large multi-family office can provide a number of skilled administrative services. See, for example, the multi-family office of Pitcairn, which promotes on its website that it is glad to be the back office partner of an SFO. We predict that these 'private label' family offices will become more prevalent. You and your family could spend some instructive time interviewing a number of those offices willing to provide back office services.

Cons: You remain a client of a family office with a number of other clients and may therefore need to understand the priority attaching to investment opportunities and how your needs fit with their other clients' needs as part of an overall workflow.

4. The need for a family office

Has there been a liquidity event that produced, or will produce, a large number of liquid assets for the family to manage, resulting in a new need?

Historically, family offices have been created to manage wealth generated from the ownership of private businesses or, in more recent times, the combined rewards of high earnings as a successful executive and long-term incentive components such as share options. However, the incidence of significant wealth realisation events over the last twenty to thirty years has been a significant contributor to the large increase in the number of new family offices. Funds generated from the sale of an operating business or the realisation of equity in a public company represent a transformation of capital and the nature of the wealth held, and are usually new territory for the successful entrepreneur.

As Figure 1 illustrates, capital transformation events bring with them a change, not only in the nature of the owner's relationship to that wealth but also in the nature of the decision making that surrounds it.

Figure 1. The evolution of family wealth

Family in business ('active wealth')	Capital transformation ('active wealth creates passive capital')	Financial family ('capital is held intergenerationally')	Business family ('active management of passive wealth')
• Reinvestment or earnings • Liquidity • Ownership • Succession • Leadership • Creation and development	• Development of social capital • Diversification of financial capital • Diverse ownership • Distributions • Sale of business assets	• Entrepreneurship • Stewardship • Leadership development – human capital • Family commitment • Risk management • Governance	• Revised ownership structures • New business development • Commitment to family ownership • Transition of leadership • Realignment of family values
Need for improved reporting and compliance	Need for different approach to wealth and risk management	Generational change requires planning and strategy	Sustainability requires governance and oversight

As the top row illustrates, the first transformation is typically from wealth represented by the ownership of an active asset like a family business, to wealth held in a more liquid form, as passive capital. This doesn't necessarily mean that the whole of the wealth is transformed; it could be that the business is so successful it generates capital in excess of its needs, and wealth in the form of dividends and distributions accrues to the owners and needs to be reinvested, with proper thought given to how it is managed.

Invariably at this point the wealth owner and their family are faced with a need to manage an increase in reporting and compliance obligations, as the number and type of legal structures deployed to manage their capital increases.

And as the amount of passive capital accumulates, so the complexity associated with its management increases, and with that the need for the family to rethink their approach to management of risk. This may involve thinking strategically about the nature of the risks facing the family and how those risks can be managed.

"For many, contemplating setting up a family office only occurs after the realisation of their active assets. Such an event is normally preceded by significant planning to maximise the value realised from the sale, and minimise the impact of taxation; but including within that planning how to manage the wealth that is realised, and specifically the possible role and structure of the family office, will reap great long-term benefits."

For some, the primary risk is preserving capital, so thought will need to be given to mitigating the risk of the value of their wealth decreasing because of market movements or poor investment decisions.

Over time, naturally, the number of family members affected directly or indirectly by the management of the passive capital increases. With this transformation comes the transition of passive capital derived by one generation into capital owned for the benefit of descendent generations and what many advisers have referred to as the 'financial family'.[9] Ensuring that wealth owned by the family remains in their collective control and ownership requires planning and strategic thinking.

Finally, there is metamorphosis into a 'business family' whose role is the management of the family's wealth in a businesslike fashion – at which point the transformation from a family business to a business family becomes complete.

Through this process the family office becomes an integral component of the family's wealth management scheme, focusing initially on the investment and management of financial capital and ultimately on management of the family's overall capital, including that attributable to:

- the value of the family members themselves (human capital);
- their engagement in their community (social capital); and
- their accumulated wisdom (intellectual capital).

For many, contemplating setting up a family office only occurs after the realisation of their active assets. Such an event is normally preceded by significant planning to maximise the value realised from the sale, and minimise the impact of taxation; but including within that planning how to manage the wealth that is realised, and specifically the possible role and structure of the family office, will reap great long-term benefits.

5. It's not all about assets

One of the most common questions we are asked is: How much wealth does a family need to own in order to think about setting up a family office? Not surprisingly, the answer is not as straightforward as you might expect.

Some say the threshold should be at least $50 million in assets, others as much as $250 million; but the most commonly quoted figure, according to Russ Allan Prince, is $100 million, that sum being sufficient to offer a cost benefit to the family in managing the money themselves as against using a third-party investment manager.[10]

However, to break the answer down into a simple cost–benefit analysis is perhaps to over-simplify the question. For example, investment management is but one element of the costs associated with the administration and management of wealth in general. Other costs include legal and professional services fees, which can all be effectively insourced. We'll be examining the nature of family office costs later in this report.

In addition, there may be other reasons besides cost for arranging an office to look after the family's interests, including direct financial benefits and broader benefits like maximising the value of the family's overall capital. We touched briefly above on how many successful families spend more time on maximising the value of the family's human and social capital through deployment of funds towards education of family members, and philanthropy, than on managing their financial capital. A family office can provide the framework for forums on these matters.

Again, some family offices exist for the primary purpose of maintaining the family's name and reputation across generations through the shared responsibility of managing a family foundation.

Finally, the level of complexity of the family's affairs may mean there is benefit in having one central point of contact to coordinate the administration of the family's affairs, perhaps resulting in short-term cost benefits but ultimately providing longer-term planning benefits by ensuring that the family's estate plans are consistent and congruent with the vision to manage the family's wealth for future generations.

In conclusion, there is no hard and fast level at which it becomes beneficial for a family to set up their own private office. Granted, it probably makes sense financially where there is a significant amount of capital that can derive economic benefits from scale and efficiency, but establishing a family office can offer far more than that.

6. The benefits of having a family office

Essentially, what the family office should offer is a sense of control; a feeling that you will be able to put your finger on all the different aspects that affect your ownership of wealth, not in the sense of being able to change the nature of the risks attaching to ownership, but of being able to more confidently manage them in order to preserve, manage, grow and diversify the family's capital.

We mentioned control, but the letter 'C' offers several other descriptors of the benefits families seek to achieve through their family office:

Figure 2. Benefits of a family office

Any or all of these benefits, to a greater or lesser degree, may be relevant to your own and your family's situation.

"Essentially, what the family office should offer is a sense of control; a feeling that you will be able to put your finger on all the different aspects that affect your ownership of wealth."

IV. Preliminary matters

Before getting too immersed in the design process, bear in mind that you might already have a functional family office in place, albeit showing signs of the stresses highlighted in chapter III.

Many families who own a business use the services of employees for personal assistance. In many cases this informal arrangement amounts to the functioning of a family office; and indeed it is now referred to as an 'embedded' family office. Eventually, for tax and other reasons, it makes sense to discontinue this "free" use of executives within the business and to separate out personal family services by forming an actual family office.

Even without an operating business, many families have developed adviser and personal assistant roles and relationships over the years, which together cover many of the services of a family office. At some point, however, the services become so numerous and the various functions so uncoordinated that the family becomes susceptible to financial loss through negligence or fraud.

We will assume that after discussion with your advisers and family, and any friends who may have taken the step of establishing their own office, you have determined that for the reasons explored above, having a family office dedicated to the needs of your family makes sense.

1. The nature of the capital to be managed

As a first step, it's worth gaining an understanding of the status quo by asking the following questions:

- What wealth does the family own?
- How is the wealth of the family held?
- What are the current costs of managing the family's wealth, including direct third-party costs and any indirect costs that may be subsidised by the family business?

A good place to start can be any documentation and materials that supported you in the development of your estate planning and testamentary provision. Your lawyer and accountant will naturally be helpful in this audit process.

It may be that there are certain assets you own that you don't want the family office to manage on your behalf. These could include your home and any lifestyle assets that may or may not be used by the family as a whole.

Assuming that the family agree in principle that there is a benefit in being collective owners of wealth – that is, in becoming a financial family – agreeing what is and is not a family asset is vital for the effective management of the family portfolio and agreeing what the family office does for its members. Absent agreement on these issues, conflict could arise between family members given their varying expectations of the family office.

In this regard, the family's capital should not be considered simply by reference to its financial resources. What can be overlooked (and therefore undervalued) are the various other types of capital that a family may own – your own networks and professional relationships and your membership of associations, for example. These can usefully add to the pool of resources that can be called upon. Indeed, your contacts may be useful to you as you consider the staffing of the family office and decide which services may be outsourced to third-party providers, and which insourced within the family office.

Perhaps most importantly, you and your family are the human capital that can be deployed by the family office. Don't underestimate the value of your human capital and the skills, experience and know-how of individual family members. Think about what skillsets exist inside the family and as far as possible identify how those skills may be deployed – it may be that this influences how much you choose to outsource. For example, someone with an accounting background can play a vital role in underpinning the financial foundations by establishing accounting and reporting procedures. Alternatively,

"You and your family are the human capital that can be deployed by the family office. Don't underestimate the value of your human capital and the skills, experience and know-how of individual family members."

someone with investment management experience may be useful in establishing rules around the management of capital, substantially reducing third-party costs.

Having a good understanding of the extent and depth of the family's overall capital is the first step to determining how best to utilise those resources within your family office.

2. The purpose of your family office

It will be useful to document the basis of your decision to start a family office. At some point you may need to confirm why the family office was set up in the first place, and what you see as being the main role of the family's wealth – perhaps as part of a regular review of the office's operations, the introduction of new family members, the marriage of children or the passing of a senior elder of the family.

Quite often families do this through the development of a shared purpose or mission statement, encompassing a broad range of aspirations of which more than one may be relevant:

- They may see the opportunity for the family to be financially secure for the rest of their lives and their descendants' lives, if the wealth is properly managed.

- They may reflect on whether there would be a significant marginal benefit in accumulating more wealth.
- They may take the view that the wealth should be applied towards enhancing the family's social capital through philanthropy or by providing resources to support a meaningful and useful education for family members.
- They may want to encourage entrepreneurship amongst family members by offering opportunities to invest in their ideas.
- They may feel that a family office will help separate the family from the business (see Figure 3 below).

Whatever your family decides is the best expression of its shared purpose, make sure that this purpose is recognised and respected by the family as a whole. The mission statement can then be used to explore the role of the family office in detail.

For a close-knit family, the mission statement might be simple:

> *To preserve our family's wealth so that it can be applied to enhance the wellbeing of our family members.*

Figure 3. Improving lines of communication around the important issues

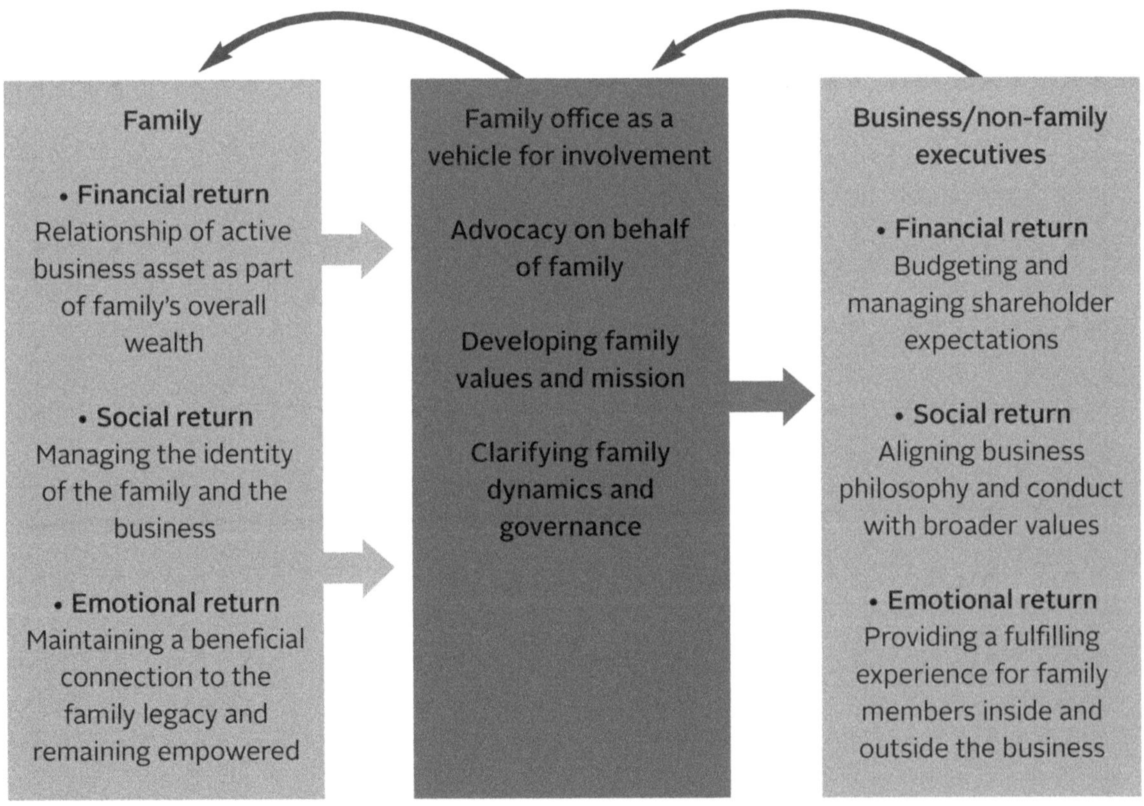

Or, this is how one SFO defines its mission:

> *MFI is a provider of long-term, patient and supportive capital and its investments are designed to support the financial future of the family and its philanthropic pursuits.*[11]

Figure 3 demonstrates how a family office is typically deployed by a family with an operating business. The family office provides a conduit between family and business for communicating what is important to the family in terms of its value system – particularly important where the growth of the business has meant that family participation has become diluted compared to that of owners.

3. The scope of the family office

Fundamentally, the family office should do what is necessary to ensure that the family's shared purpose is delivered and its mission achieved.

If the shared purpose is to preserve wealth for the benefit of the family and subsequent 'blood' descendants, and to provide for their education and wellbeing, then the family may adopt a long-term approach to managing family capital, reduce as far as possible the impact of consumption and costs as leakages from the portfolio and work on how family wellbeing can be defined and ultimately delivered.

You can see here that the definition of 'purpose' becomes extremely important and your family will benefit from ensuring that this has been discussed thoroughly at the outset. It is possible, for example, that there will be an ambition for the family office to do specific, purposeful things such as engaging in philanthropic endeavours through the establishment of a private foundation.

Being very explicit on what the family office will and won't do can be particularly useful where you employ staff to supply services to the family. We talk about this more fully in chapter V, "Starting the process".

4. Will the family play a role?

This might seem like an odd question, but it is not necessarily a given that your family will play a role in the family office. What is without question, of course, is that the family office exists solely to meet the needs of your family.[12]

There are some key questions that you might want to think about in considering how the family would work with the family office.

- Do you see yourself as being able to work alongside your family in managing the family's wealth?

"Understanding the extent to which a family member is willing to tie their destiny to the family is key to the design of the family office and the nature of what it does and how it thinks about the management of family capital."

- To what extent would you like your children to be involved in managing the family capital in the future?

Agreeing to work together as a family provides significant opportunities in the context of economic empowerment, cost-efficient services, access leverage and social connections – but all family members will need to agree on the benefits. Whilst the benefits may be obvious, particularly the financial ones, be aware that there may also be responsibilities and accountabilities that need to be adopted.

Whether your family plays a role will be dependent upon what the family office is set up to achieve and the relevant skills and experience that family members possess.

It is not generally a wise idea simply to create a position for a family member inside a family office, without there being a clearly defined role. In your own business, or in any professional services environment, you will know that it is better to have the right people in the right roles. The audit you've conducted of your family's capital will help here.

It is also a good idea that, having agreed a shared purpose, the family should be engaged in the design process as far as possible, and in this context the family may wish to ask the question: Who is the family office for? Being very clear as to who the family office serves is extremely important. Should its services extend to parents, siblings, nephews and nieces or even further to aunts, uncles and cousins? At some point it may well be that the family office will serve not just your own needs and those of your children, but also the needs of their families.

What is meant by 'family' is typically determined by the founder's family relationships. A lot can be inferred by checking the beneficiaries of pre-existing structures such as family discretionary trusts. Again, the pre-planning you've done to understand your current situation will be extremely helpful in this regard.

Questions you may want to ask yourself as the founder are:

- How important is your own financial independence from other family members?
- Do you want to consult with family members on matters affecting the family?

For family members, being able to provide for one's family independently can be important in developing self-esteem, and many create their own financial plan with the fruit of the family's capital tree. Accordingly, don't be surprised if some family members do not choose to be a part of the family office.

Understanding the extent to which a family member is willing to tie their destiny to the family is key to the design of the family office and the nature of what it does and how it thinks about the management of family capital.

It is probably best in the first instance to set up the family office to meet your own direct family's needs, and then to widen the number of those entitled to use its services, as appropriate.

V. Starting the process

As we have explained, a family office is typically formed as a consequence of the need to reconsider how to manage the family's capital following the sale, in whole or in part, of an operating business. Up to that point, many of the service needs of the business owner will probably have been served by head office, in the business' accounting function, while others may have been fulfilled by external service providers.

In creating a family office, it is therefore important to understand:

- how the balance between in-house and external provision has operated in the past;
- what is working; and
- what service needs are missing.

Usually, when the decision has been made, there is a migration from the business office infrastructure to a more formalised family office structure. Depending on the nature of the sale event, this could mean that certain staff are retained and transferred into the family office.

1. The priorities

In this scenario, a fairly well-defined set of tasks and activities will have been undertaken on your behalf in the past; and in fleshing out the needs of the family for the future it is worth asking, What priorities should the family focus on now?

Table 2 breaks these priorities down into short-, medium- and long-term.

Table 2. Summary of priorities

Short term	By first understanding • the nature of the assets owned (the What); • the structure of ownership (the How); • and your own feelings around being financially comfortable (the Why) it is possible to develop a plan for the future evolution and management of the wealth at hand.
Medium term	• The plan should be informed by your own current needs and objectives, including lifestyle needs and expectations. • It is best practice to give thought to how the plan, once determined, is communicated to those likely to be affected.
Long term	On the basis that your plan provides for the joint ownership of wealth for the benefit of your descendants, the process by which control and oversight will operate needs to be carefully considered – specifically: • how the family will combine as joint decision makers; and • whether the role of independent decision makers, acting on the family's behalf, will be relevant.

1.1 Short term (first three months)

During the first three months it will be useful to ensure that you, or those you've recruited, have:

- completed an audit of the family's capital and the skills and resources available to use as a family;
- determined whether all compliance and regulatory obligations are up to date, including accounting for the recent sale of the business or other liquidity event;
- confirmed that all financial commitments have been met and processes put in place to meet ongoing obligations of the family;
- examined pre-existing systems and processes put in place to meet day-to-day needs and functions, and considered how they should be changed – including the extent to which pre-existing banking relationships should be maintained;

"A key point is that management of the financial capital is not, at this stage, the most important item on the agenda: without family buy-in to the idea of a family office and the commitment it is likely to entail, it would be easy for family members to disengage, or not to participate in the first place."

- mapped all legal relationships entered into by the family as a whole and gained an understanding of their role and purpose; and
- considered your own attitude to financial independence.

1.2 Medium term (twelve to eighteen months)
Having established the various documents, structures and relationships that underpin the family's wealth and how it is maintained, the next few months should be given over to engaging with the family on the business plan and strategy for the family office:

- The basis for the family office and its purpose should be discussed, agreed and set out.
- The family should define the role of the family office and develop a strategy to manage its functions and obligations.
- A plan should be developed and communicated to the family for the ongoing management of the family's capital over the long term.

A key point is that management of the financial capital is not, at this stage, the most important item on the agenda: without family buy-in to the idea of a family office and the commitment it is likely to entail, it would be easy for family members to disengage, or not to participate in the first place.

1.3 Long term (continuing obligations)

The history of successful family wealth transitions points to the two main indicia of success as being trust and communication.[13] To be successful, a family needs to develop a forum for effective decision making and have that forum coordinated on its behalf. Traditionally, this has been a role for the family office, whose success will ultimately be determined by how it communicates with the family and builds trust across generations.

There is a great deal that can be done to shore up the family office proposition in the minds of your family members through regular communication and having an effective governance structure in place (see chapter XIII).

Those running the family office need to be conscious of meeting its objectives, which will typically include the following:

- preserving family capital over the long term;
- educating the family around the purpose of the family's wealth;
- helping the family to manage their own financial affairs expectations; and
- helping family members to understand the balance between consumption and reinvestment and the implications on their long-term future of getting it wrong.

All of which requires that there be some form of governance and oversight of the family office.

Over the long term, planning, reviewing and reforming how the family's needs will be met by the family office will be a necessary and vitally important function.

VI. What will the family office look like?

As illustrated in Figure 4 below, the family office acts as a hub, bringing together and coordinating the various advisers. In normal circumstances, family members deal directly only with the family office. Multiple additional disciplines could be added, but the advice of seasoned family offices is to start small and grow organically as needed.

Figure 4. The family office as a coordinator of services

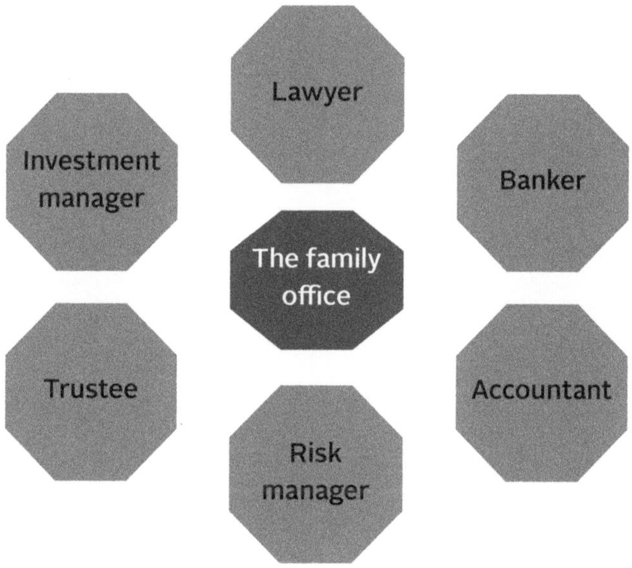

In the rush to join his peers who already had family offices, one man called us, and with no other background information said, "I read your article. I want one. How many square feet should I buy in Manhattan?"

As with the sister question, "How much does an SFO cost?", we always have the same response: "It depends."

The three most important considerations are the services to offer; the location; and the name.

1. Services

The family must decide which services they most want to include – on the understanding that other services can be added later. That decision will determine which staff to hire and with what backgrounds and skills. Hiring staff for a family office is much different to hiring staff for an investment firm, as we will discuss later. Knowing the type and number of staff will determine the size of the required space, which will round out the calculation of the cost of running the office.

2. Location

Many families choose locations away from home, for reasons we will discuss in chapter VIII below.[14] Some decide to split the office into two jurisdictions. For example, a family in the Middle East chose their home area for the family office that would provide personal services, and London as the site where the investments would be managed.

3. Name

Most families value their privacy and do not put their name in the name of the family office. Instead they choose something that has meaning to the family but is not descriptive in a public sense. We know two families who chose the name of a favourite vacation spot, and a number who used a combination of some letters of the names of family members. One example that brought the generations together nicely was to defer to the younger generation to choose the name. The process engendered a great sense of belonging.

VII. What will the family office do?

The list of services that a family office may provide is extensive; indeed, it is possible for the whole of a family's needs to be met by an SFO provided it has the necessary resources, as well as skills within the family, to do so.

The crucial question is whether to 'build' or to 'buy'. That's to say:

- What services will be insourced (delivered by the family office)?
- What services will be outsourced (delivered by a third-party agent)?

1. To build or to buy?
In this context it will be helpful to ask:

- What is the depth of the family's management capability?
- How are the family's skillsets complementary to the family's management needs?
- Is the family's wealth seen as a separate business requiring hands-on management?

Commonly, those services that an office within the family business used to deliver on behalf of the family are easy to transfer across to the new family office. Typically they will include paying bills, keeping books and accounts and liaising with the family accountant on tax returns and related filings.

Likewise, those services that are more personal to the family and relate to the management and upkeep of personal or lifestyle assets may also be better delivered by the family office.

Thereafter, it will be the nature of the capital that requires management that will to a large extent determine whether the family office chooses to insource or outsource; and in the case of investment management it may well be a combination of both that provides the solution the family needs.

2. Investment management and oversight
Investment management is often seen as the primary purpose of setting up a family office. It is not straightforward to decide how to manage investments and retain appropriate family oversight. Investment professionals are expensive hires. The family needs to choose between build or buy in this area. We know one SFO that has hired an investment professional at his market salary but has kept costs down by his creating only two funds for the family to choose from: one income and one growth.

In most cases the family office has a chief investment officer (CIO) who selects and monitors the highly paid outside professionals. Keeping the family involved is sometimes difficult, but we stress that there does need to be a degree of family oversight, especially to prevent fraud.

We find it useful for generational planning to include one or more members of the younger generation on an investment committee for purposes of direct education and input.

Finally, we think that those family offices where the sole function is the investment function are more correctly described as private investment firms.

3. Cash flow management and projections
Everyone knows the expression, "rich on paper but cash-poor". This can be addressed by careful projections and cash flow management – another valued service offered by the family office team. We have heard too many tales of billionaires never understanding what their cash needs might be in the short or even the long term.

4. Consolidated financial reports
For many years the fervent wish of family offices was to find and use consolidated financial reporting. Financial firms would provide their

own style of reports, and the different firms could seldom combine their reporting to give the family an accurate overall picture. Financial reporting has improved, but still often fails to take into account the non-financial assets, which require separate valuations.

5. Budget preparation, for all family members

Most individuals do better if they are able to make financial plans for themselves. Part of that is budget preparation, which is helpful no matter the extent of the family wealth. Particularly for generational planning, it is helpful to forecast the increase in number of family members and their call on the family wealth. In one family office an outside investment consultant was able to demonstrate to a "spendthrift" family member that the current spending pattern was unsustainable.[15]

6. Bank financing

A family office is often able to minimise bank charges, partly as a result of its ability to introduce a larger group of family members as customers, and partly through the hope that future family members will also sign on. We know of one billionaire who told his bank that because of the goodwill the bank received from having him as a customer, it should be willing to lend him money at zero interest.

7. Residences management

Many family members with family offices also own more than one home. Without the family office these are managed on an individual basis without a lot of oversight, in our experience. Among the functions of a family office can be to hire, train, oversee and replace household staff. We know one family office based in the United States where the only duty was to manage six households in Europe, complete with nannies in each location. Household staff need to be screened and background checks are essential, as are confidentiality agreements. Some family offices are also charged with moving wardrobes from location to location, and there are services that will mark and move such collections.

8. Yacht and aircraft management

Purchasing a yacht or aircraft is a significant event and a specialised lawyer should be consulted. Yachts and aircraft need maintenance staff and crew, as well as specialised risk managers or insurers. It seems that, especially for aircraft, the family office ends up having to keep track of which family member should be 'charged' for usage. For yachts we have not heard similar concerns. In one family office, also connected to a business, the yacht is clearly used for business development purposes. In another family office the yacht is used for family gatherings. In Hong Kong one patriarch commented to us that although the rest of the world found his yacht to be on the ostentatious side he enjoyed using it for family gatherings – he said they couldn't leave in the middle of proceedings.

9. Art collection management

Art (and other) collections are challenging in several respects. At the time of purchase it is critical to receive a solid written provenance. Pieces must have specialised insurance. Storage must meet certain conditions. When possible, a piece should have an estimated market value and be listed on the family's consolidated balance sheet. If a piece is being moved there are special concerns.[16] For sales and acquisitions the family office should develop a good working relationship with one of the major auction houses, and if the owner intends for the collection to remain in family hands, a specialised private client lawyer should be consulted.

10. Risk management procedures and policies

For a fuller discussion of risk management, see chapter XI, "Managing risk". This is an area that is easily overlooked, yet it can be the cause of substantial harm to the family and to their investments. With a new family office there is often a tendency to be casual. We know of many instances where the controls were not in place to prevent a wire fund transfer supposedly by a family member that was in fact fraudulent. Authorisations should be spelled out clearly and monitored professionally, including through regular audits.

10.1 Health and life insurance

In addition to ensuring that each family member has appropriate life and medical insurance, some family offices are joining global networks that provide preventive and wellbeing benefits.[17]

10.2 Personal security, including kidnap and ransom coverage

In terms of risk, one of the most serious – and most feared – is the risk of physical danger or kidnap for ransom. We recommend that the family members meet with one of the specialist firms in this field to learn about safer behaviour. It is smart to develop an emergency plan, so that if a kidnap happens the family office knows who to contact and how to access substantial sums of money if appropriate.

10.3 Reputational risk and social media policies

Although it does not have the gravity of physical risk, today the risk of damage to a family's reputation through the use of social media is increasingly important. In the event of reputational threat, the family office can act as spokesperson for the family. All family members should be schooled in the safe use of social media.

11. Coordination of estate planning and life insurance

Our recommendation is that the family office gather every single signed

"It is smart to develop an emergency plan, so that if a kidnap happens the family office knows who to contact and how to access substantial sums of money if appropriate."

estate planning document and either review them or ask an outside professional to review them. We often recommend that the family office stage a 'fire drill' with the scenario of the surprise death of a patriarch:

- What would happen?
- Who would receive what funds?
- Who would be in charge of the office?
- Who would the successor trustees be?
- Who would have the authority to deal with financial institutions, etc?

12. Bill-paying
Often one of the first functions a family office takes over is everyday bill-paying. We have seen this handled by way of a simple carrying out of family directions or a more comprehensive gathering and analysing of bills, with an eye on any unusual items.

13. Reporting and compliance
Reporting and compliance in response to regulatory requirements has become an important task for family office staff, for tasks as simple as opening bank accounts, making tax declarations and other official reporting. The family office should be able to provide the family with the privacy it needs, while taking away admin burdens.

14. Hiring, overseeing and firing

14.1 Household staff

Especially if there is more than one residence it can become very challenging to recruit, oversee and fire household staff. The family office can easily take over this role. Informal networks can be a source of candidates for posts from nanny to butler. It will be important to have all the staff sign strict confidentiality agreements. The more 'public' the family is, the more important is the confidentiality of the staff.

14.2 Other staff

Beyond household staff, the family office can be the main liaison office for handling all sorts of service providers and experts the family might need to address legal, financial and lifestyle matters.

15. Record-keeping

Having a central office as custodian of important contracts, documents related to family decisions, investments, transactions, legal and compliance dossiers, is an undervalued but crucial function of a family office. Geographically dispersed multi-generation families need a reliable repository with both physical and virtual storage.

The temptation in new offices is to be somewhat casual, but this can cause problems later. No one should have to spend time searching for records. It will be worth allocating time to maintaining central electronic copies of all important records, and more than one person should know how to locate them.

16. Tax returns and projections

Some family offices have the internal ability to prepare all of the relevant tax returns. More often, though, we find that this is a function that is delegated to an outside accounting firm. Those who prepare the returns also need to explain them to the family members, and to prepare projections of estimated future taxes.

17. Trust oversight

In the United States and other common law jurisdictions, notably England, Canada and Australia, clients who are wealthy are likely to have a number of trusts. These can accumulate over the years. A smart practice is for someone to prepare very short summaries of the key provisions of each document (such as ages or standards for distributions, and directions about investments and the selection process for successor trustees) to be sure that they do not contradict each other and that they correspond to the wishes of the family.[18]

18. Philanthropy

Philanthropy is often an active area for all family members. When there is a family office it can be of help in a number of ways. At an individual level the family office can research the charities of interest to a family member and help monitor the charity's use of family funds. At a combined family level the office can help with the creation of a family charity foundation, or donor-advised fund. Some family offices organise annual visits to charities supported by the family. Working together on philanthropic activities is often valued as a bonding activity for a family as well as being an educational vehicle for younger family members.

19. Family education

There is a maxim that wealth is lost in three generations. The antidote is often said to be to keep the family strong and together, generation after generation. See the discussion on governance in chapter XIII. Families with accumulated wealth often worry that the younger generations will not be equipped to handle the wealth responsibly – hence the proliferation of programmes on 'responsible wealth' or 'wealth stewardship'. Next-generation families should be offered an insight into family history and the family business, and indeed if they are not specifically educated about managing wealth they are at risk. Resources should be formally allocated for these purposes, and

"There is a maxim that wealth is lost in three generations. The antidote is often said to be to keep the family strong and together, generation after generation."

perhaps seed funding for business and investment ideas. This can help identify roles in the business and/or family office for interested and qualified family members. We know one older family office in the United States that has decided to delegate almost all other functions in order to focus on the education of the younger family members. Another large SFO has hired a full-time education director whose function is to keep the many family members informed about the activities of the operating companies, in an effort to create wise owners in the next generation. One Swiss consultant is retained by family offices to train the younger generation on how to hire and evaluate investment managers. The breadth and content of the education programmes vary by family.

20. Family meetings

As part of keeping the family together, we recommend that the family office take over the function of organising regular family meetings. We also recommend that an outside facilitator be hired to conduct those meetings. Several years ago at a New York private gathering of families with family offices the question was asked: Can you have good family meetings without a facilitator? Everyone laughed and the answer was, No! One reason for this is that it is difficult for a family member to function in two roles simultaneously – as a participating family member and as a leader of the meeting. Another negative is that family members will have developed their own roles over the years, and family meetings may involve a change in roles and power structure.

We have served as facilitator in a number of meetings, and are careful to sit at the head of the table and take charge, making sure that each family member has a fair opportunity to participate. Families of all sizes can benefit immensely from a tradition of open, regular meetings.

21. Lifestyle and concierge services

Finally, there is the function of family concierge service. This is the luxury service of having staff available to just take care of everything.

Event planning is in this category. For family events – weddings, births, graduations, birthdays, and other celebrations – the family office can help organise the events, either directly or by hiring outside event professionals. We know one family in Europe that hires a Swiss chateau for a month each summer to strengthen family ties, have meetings and just have fun.

Some families enjoy sharing their travel plans and experiences, and their office might create a private website for that purpose – in addition, of course, to handling travel arrangements. If there is a private jet, or yacht, the office can be responsible for handling the various requests for use.

For some, this is one of the more enjoyable parts of working in a family office – the requests can come in a surprising variety. One request was to find the artist who painted a piece that a family member saw in a hotel during a holiday, and try to source another piece by the same artist. One family member, explaining how important the family office was to him, said that on his passport page asking who to contact in an emergency he had listed the family office.

On the other hand, some family offices that are focused on investments clearly think that concierge services are beneath them. They announce, "We do not walk the dog." There is an interesting range of attitudes on the subject and you will be free to choose the services your family would like to have.

VIII. Location

Jan van Bueren and Thomas Ming have provided an excellent framework of issues to consider when choosing the location of your SFO. A detailed discussion is beyond the scope of this report, but the following heads are from their 12-point list:[19]

- Where will support be required?
- Where do the family members live? Are they all in the same jurisdiction (this is increasingly unlikely)?
- Where are the assets located?
- Where will staff and executives be needed?
- What is the quality of the local infrastructure and expertise?
- What legal forms of SFO are available in the jurisdiction under consideration?
- What if any are the licences and regulations that would apply?
- What are the taxes and other costs?
- How stable, politically and economically, is the jurisdiction?
- How experienced is the jurisdiction in data protection and privacy?

We would also add: How safe is the jurisdiction? Risk of kidnapping, for example, can be an important concern in some jurisdictions.

There are other practical factors if several jurisdictions are possible, such as the convenience of being in similar time zones, ease of travel to the jurisdiction and visa requirements.

IX. Staffing

It is estimated that approximately 60% of the costs of an SFO are related directly to salaries and benefits paid to staff.[20]

1. Recruitment

Finding the right staff for your family office is probably the most important of all tasks to be completed. It may be that you first need to identify a consultant to help in your thinking about the purpose and role of the family office, rather than diving straight into recruitment.

It is likely that the first employees of the family office have been working for you within your business for some time. This is because not only is the wealth typically generated from the sale of that business, but these people will probably have been intimately involved with the finance function of the business, its pre-existing processes and the network of professional relationships that have been built.

However, dependent upon the specific needs of the new family office, there will be a requirement to identify suitable employees.

A family office management role is unlike a position in a public financial firm – the job description is often unclear and, even if clear, might not match the expectations of the family.

One family office recruiting firm with a UK base stresses the importance of matching the culture of the office with the right recruit:[21]

> *This is a workplace where it's more than just business, it's personal; you're recruiting into a team that is managing, growing and protecting family assets. It's an environment where the people may be required to go above, beyond, below and beside what their job title suggests is within their remit.*

Tips for long-term hires

Rankin Group's MJ Rankin offers this recruitment advice:[22]

- Develop a formal hiring process. Commit necessary time to defining your culture and the success criteria for prospective candidates.
- Write a well-defined job description that relates to the company's goals and objectives and expectations for the person in this role.
- Set a competitive, market-valued compensation for the job.
- Interview more than one candidate and look beyond the résumé to determine cultural and behavioural fit with the organisation and other members of the team.
- Hire candidates who are not just like you, but complement your skills, experience and style.
- Follow through on background and reference checks. Be sure you know who you are hiring.
- Promise a candidate only what you can deliver.
- Have others in the organisation/family interview the candidate(s).
- Don't rely on classified or internet advertising.
- Network to keep tabs on the hiring pool in anticipation of future needs; develop internal bench strength when you can.

Some recruiters emphasise a battery of personality profile tests. In our experience it is also effective to evaluate candidates in several interviews.

Focus first on hiring the head of the office, then include that person in the recruitment process for other key staff.

Finally, we always advise clients to start small and add staff as and when needed.

2. Remuneration
Getting the remuneration structure of the family office right is often problematic. There are several reasons for this, not least that you are searching in a professional market of talented individuals who may, depending on the role you are looking to fill, have been engaged under lucrative contracts.

Clearly, the nature of the role and what is sought to be delivered will be determinants as regards an individual's expectations.

As a general rule, remuneration levels inside family offices are affected by issues of complexity and scale. A number of surveys of the sector across different geographies suggest that the amount of the assets under management tends to correlate with the salaries offered.

Amongst the challenges are the fact that executives on your target list of candidates will probably have several components to their existing salary package, including both short- and long-term incentives (STIs and LTIs).

Whether you can match these salary components depends on the resources available, which will be dictated to a large extent by the

"You may be able to offer unique allowances and fringe benefits to potential employees that are outside those ordinarily available, and it is conceivable that the culture you exude and your vision for the role may be compelling."

planning that has been undertaken for the running of the office. This may or may not rule out some targets based on a candidate's existing position.

STIs are typically cash-based bonus structures and so could conceivably be structured into a family office staff member's salary package.

In the case of public markets, LTIs typically involve offering equity rights in consideration for meeting certain goals and targets, perhaps tied to the employer's share price. It is obviously difficult for a family office to offer a similar incentive.

Instead, the nature of any LTI component will be a function of the value that the role adds relative to the purpose of the family office. In the case of investment professionals, the LTI may be an offering of co-investment rights alongside the family in direct investment opportunities. The important thing is that it is not beyond the capacity of a family office to offer LTIs that are of value to the recipient.

A great deal, however, will depend on what the individual is looking for and on developing a holistic approach to the setting of the remuneration structure.[23] You may, for example, be able to offer a far more attractive, lifestyle-orientated engagement where there is greater freedom in the way that the individual is required to meet their work obligations.

You may be able to offer unique allowances and fringe benefits to potential employees that are outside those ordinarily available, and it is conceivable that the culture you exude and your vision for the role may be compelling.

X. Cost of running the family office

How much does running a family office cost? It is one of the commonest questions but perhaps the most difficult to answer prescriptively. Much depends on what services the family needs, how best those services can be delivered, and how much the family can afford.

Frequently, the family office is created following receipt of a significant financial windfall, be it the proceeds of sale of a business or the takeover of a listed stock. The proceeds have replaced the previous source of the family's income and distributions, and it is quite probable that you and your family will not receive a similar large sum of money again.

Whereas you could confidently have expected to receive an annual dividend of £X or regular salary of £Y or, typically, a combination of both, you'll now be reliant upon the return on your capital to meet your financial needs. For this reason, owners of family businesses often hesitate to sell, arguing that the return on capital the business generates could not be matched by the management of a portfolio of investments. To a great extent this is probably true. But having received an offer that was too good to be true and absent an alternative, you made the decision to sell and now need to spend some time fully appreciating what it means to manage a portfolio of investments rather than run an operating business.

Preservation or consumption?

As it has such a bearing on cost, you will need to revisit the question: What is the purpose of my wealth? This will crystallise what the wealth is there to do, and consequently how the portfolio needs to be invested from a risk perspective to satisfy your mission statement – and at what cost.

For example, you may have established that the purpose of your wealth is to provide for the wellbeing of your family across generations, and that therefore a key requirement is that the portfolio is managed with a view to preserving capital over the long term.

Alternatively, you may see the capital as being there both to support your family's lifestyle and to enhance their life experiences, including providing the very best education. Each agreed purpose potentially requires a different approach to the management of the capital, and more importantly involves a different financial burden, the second being likely to cost more than the first.

In deciding, therefore, how the portfolio should be structured, the choice is between:

- managing the capital so that the family lives within its means (ie, from the return on the portfolio after tax); or
- drawing down on the capital to meet the family's preferred lifestyle needs.

The choice is rarely the latter but the actual behaviour exhibited suggests it should be. Simply put, the level of consumption has by far the biggest impact on the capacity of a portfolio to last over several generations.

Knowing how much to consume without eating into capital relies on understanding the potential return on the portfolio, which itself largely depends on the risk that the investor is willing to bear over the determined timeframe. In broad terms, the higher the risk, the higher the return over the long term. Even so, there is a limit to what may be expected as a return from a portfolio of largely passive investments.

For present purposes let's assume that you can target a real return of between four and five per cent.[24]

Assuming that the financial resources available to the family office are £100 million, the anticipated total return on that portfolio would be between £4m and £5m, a net return after tax of between £3m and £3.8m.

Assuming that your own living needs and those of your family are £2m per annum, this leaves approximately £1m to £2m to run the family office over the year, including all third-party costs and salaries.

1. Start small

Given that salaries and third-party investment management fees account for such a high proportion of family office running costs, it makes sense to start small, focusing on key service needs by transplanting into the family office the existing services you and your family use.

This strategy provides a degree of certainty – if your family office is being set up to provide services to you and your family following the sale of a family business, you will have a good idea of what costs the business used to bear in this area.

2. Benchmarking the costs

There have been numerous studies undertaken to establish the costs of running an SFO.[25] Not surprisingly, they vary across regions but in broad terms the costs of management are typically between 1.1% and 1.3% per annum of the value of the family's pool of capital, split between operating costs (excluding external management fees), investment administration fees (custody and brokerage) and investment management performance fees.

Citibank's Guide to Establishing a Family Office estimated that for a family with $155 million of assets, the annual cost of running the family office is between $1.5m and $3.3m.[26] In addition, the report offered several cost models for small, medium, large and very large offices, as shown in Figure 5.

Figure 5. Family office cost models

Family Office	Full-time professional staff	Full-time support staff	Low-end annual cost	High-end annual cost
Small	2	4	$1.5 million	$1.8 million
Medium	4	11	$3 million	$3.8 million
Large	8	16	$8 million	$10 million
Very large	16	32	$14 million	$20 million

Source: A Guide to Establishing a Family Office, © 2018 Citibank, NA. All rights reserved.

The 2019 UBS/Campden Wealth Global Family Office Report survey of over 500 SFOs and MFOs worldwide also provided the average salaries for various key roles within the family office from CEO to CFO – see Figure 6 below.[27]

Such surveys offer a relative benchmark only. It is not clear, for example, whether the CEOs covered by the UBS/Campden Wealth survey were themselves family members who might be willing to receive a restricted salary in view of any additional benefits accruing from distributions.

3. Family member funding – service costs versus contributions to corpus

It is, of course, not uncommon for the SFO to recover certain costs by charging family members for its services. Typically, this occurs when the number of generations served by the family expands to include cousins at the family's third generation. In such circumstances, the SFO may also have formal terms of engagement in place to cover the services it will provide to the family member concerned, so that no one family member subsidises the services provided to all.

Discussion on this is probably best left to a time when the SFO has

Figure 6. Base salary of key family office personnel by region (USD)

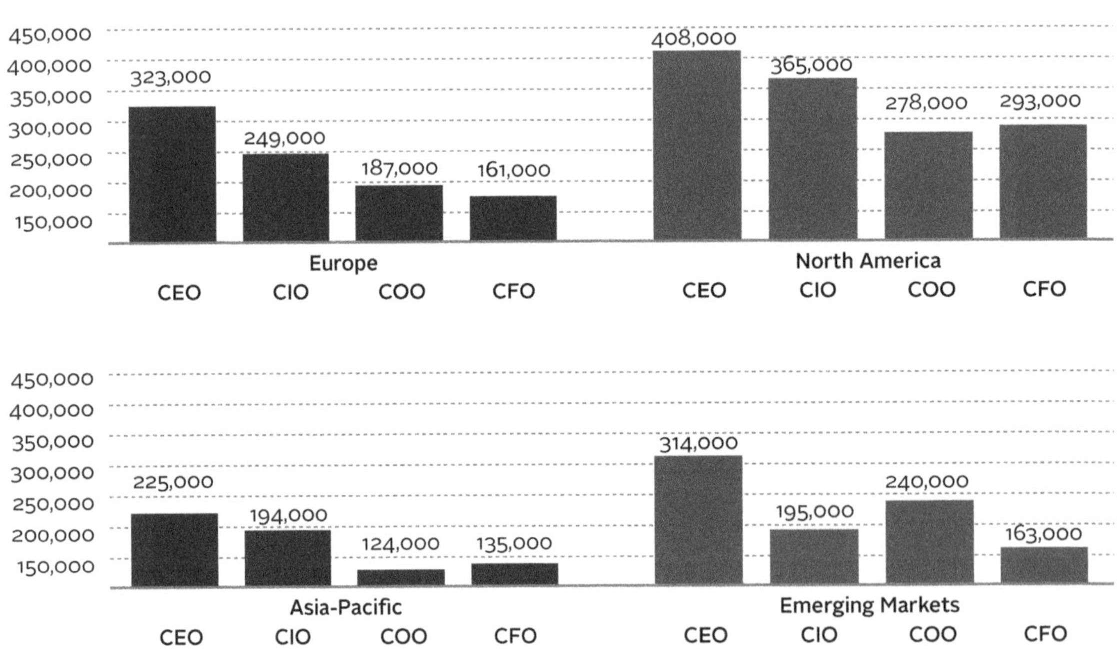

Source: UBS/Campden Wealth Global Family Office Report 2019

been up and running for a number of years and has invited a broader number of family members to become engaged with the office.

Alternative mechanisms exist to maintain the pool of the family's financial capital as the number of individuals served by the SFO increases. One such example is where family members have agreed to contribute a set percentage of their own earnings to the corpus of their family's investment capital in consideration of being able to access the benefits of the SFO and the management of the family's investments.

Under such models, the family member will accept that to continue to enjoy the benefits of the SFO there must be some mechanism that allows for the SFO to recover its costs; but by doing so the family member will probably pay less than the ordinary commercial rate.

4. Outsourced investment management

Excluding salaries, the most significant area of expense for an SFO is investment management fees. These include not just the cost of paying someone to manage the portfolio, but also the costs associated with the ownership of the assets – custody fees, administration costs associated with maintaining the family's interests in the portfolio, and the production and forwarding of relevant reports.

The range of investment management fees charged is broad, reflecting the asset class invested in, the style of management brought to bear on the portfolio and the extent to which the investment manager is rewarded by way of additional performance fee, or carry, in the case of private equity managers.

Changes in the structure of the investment management industry are having an impact on fees. Those changes include:

- the increase in the use of technology in the management of portfolios, which has reduced fund management costs;
- the rapid growth and availability of passive-style funds which offer exposure to a market (rather than individual stock selection), which has driven down overall costs of management;
- the increase in the purported alignment between fund managers and investors, resulting in lower annual management fees and keener focus on absolute returns; and
- recognition of the importance of SFOs to the funds management industry, and willingness by fund managers to offer services to SFOs at a significant discount to the rates and charges offered to retail clients in general.

Nevertheless, as illustrated by Figure 7 below, successful and consistent performance by investment managers remains highly rewarded and the cost represents a significant part of the overall costs of running an SFO.

For this reason, many SFOs may choose to outsource the investment management function to third-party managers under what is typically referred to as a 'manager of the managers' approach.[28]

Figure 7. Family offices' operating costs in basis points (SFO + MFO), 2018 and 2019

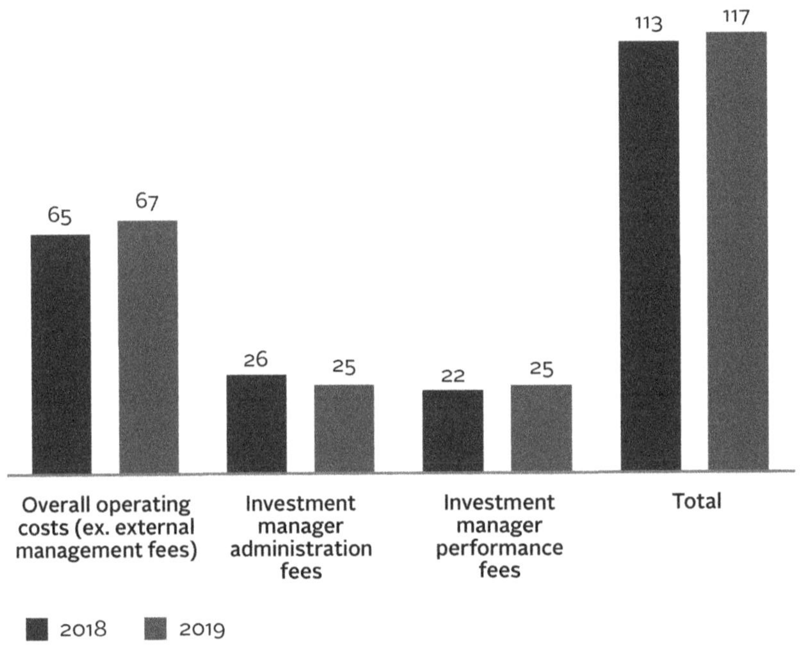

Source: UBS/Campden Wealth Global Family Office Report 2019

XI. Managing risk

It is a fundamental function of the family office to control, manage and mitigate risks on behalf of the family. Such risks, should they occur, could have both financial and non-financial consequences.

In 2006 the Family Office Exchange (FOX)[29] hosted a roundtable of family office executives in the United States. The outcome was to suggest that the family office's role should be seen primarily as helping a family to manage their risks.[30]

The key question is, What am I most worried about in relation to my wealth?

In thinking about your response, it is useful to assess risks by reference to your long-term plans and objectives.

It is likely that primary amongst the risks identified is the fear of losing money or hard-earned wealth by poor management. However, you may also be concerned to ensure that your reputation and social position is not jeopardised for any reason, and that you are protected against the increasing threat of someone accessing and stealing your personal data.

Over time, another concern may be what will happen to your wealth and its capacity to work for the benefit of your grandchildren and their children.

So, we can see that the nature of risk varies by reference to:

- the likelihood of occurrence;
- the time when risks will be most prevalent; and
- their potential impact.

Categories of risk
The risks you identify may fall into several broad categories:

Ownership and control – the risk that you and your family are no longer owners and controllers of the wealth you've created.

Family relationships – the risk that the wealth itself affects the family's personal relationships.

Wealth management – the risk that poor management will see the wealth dissipated.

Regulation and compliance – the risk that you will not meet your compliance obligations at an operational level.

Whilst these categories are necessarily general in nature you can, by being more specific, articulate the precise nature of the risks, the likelihood of them arising, and the impact should they occur. It will then be possible to develop strategies within the family office to mitigate them.

For example, if the biggest risk is miscommunication between family members, and the impact of that risk occurring would be to affect the family's financial health and overall wellbeing, then one of the key focus areas for the family office should be developing a communication forum. Such a forum would involve the whole family and help them develop their mission statement and sense of collective ownership.

At an operational level, as the family office becomes established and takes on staff it will, much like any other business, need to have regard to a broader set of risks which arise simply by virtue of being organised and employing people to look after the family's needs. A useful chart of the variety of risks at an operational level is set out in Figure 7 below, created by Linda Bourn, a partner at Crystal Alliant Private Client, a New York-based privately owned business specialising in risk management.

Figure 8. Family office risk and insurance areas

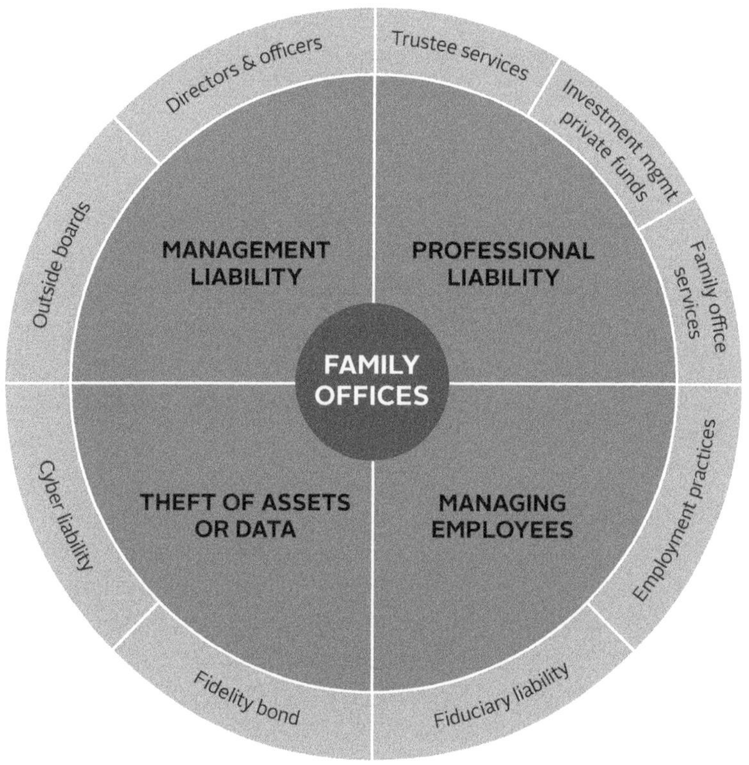

Source: Crystal Alliant Private Client

In addition, Linda recommends that a family office revisit the following key questions each year:[31]

- What are the new risks that we are facing that could have a substantial impact, and how are we addressing them?
- What plan do we have in place to protect our family office against cybercrime?[32]
- Do we have an annual review process to identify the risks to family members?
- Have we aligned our family office risk exposures with an insurance strategy?

Typical insurance programmes for family offices include the following areas:

- directors and officers and private company liability;
- errors and omissions: family office services, trustees, investment management and private funds, including vicarious liability;
- employment practices liability;
- cyber liability;
- crime insurance or fidelity bond; and
- social engineering liability.

1. Fiduciary liability
The following deserve a special mention because to some extent they require not only the attention of the family office, but the family as a whole:

- privacy;
- reputation; and
- social media.

One of the hottest issues today is developing a sound policy to protect the privacy and reputations of family members. There are a number of experts who focus on educating a family as to safe practices on social media. Law firms now have departments devoted to reputation management.

2. Kidnap risk protection
A key priority in most family offices should be to develop a 'kidnap and ransom' plan. Again, there are a number of firms that specialise in this area. They stress the value of having a plan in place, so that if such an event occurs the designated members of the team know who to contact, how to release sufficient funds, and so on.

3. Health and wellbeing
Finally, family offices are increasingly addressing the health and wellbeing of family members. Provision of comprehensive global care, particularly in the preventive care area, is still a fairly young field. Qineticare, based in Hong Kong,[33] is an example of a new firm stressing wellbeing in all its aspects.

XII. Infrastructure

It is unhelpful to be too prescriptive in terms of infrastructure. It is your office after all, and you and your family will be the best judges of how to manage your capital, the guiding principle being that a family office is run for the benefit of the family.

As with costs, starting slowly before building significant infrastructure will help pave the way for a more successful long-term office.

Figure 9 on the next page illustrates how many SFOs that are primarily responsible for managing the family's wealth are organised.

The owners sit as family board members overseeing the executive team (see chapter XIII on governance). Typically that board will include family members, perhaps just you and your spouse – it is important not to overreach on board participation, especially if just starting out.

The executive team you put together will reflect your earlier decisions as to the needs of the family. The CEO or general manager is probably the first role you'll recruit for, if you aren't going to take on that role yourself. He or she will probably come from a finance background and in many cases will already be known to you.

The right infrastructure is crucial, and it doesn't have to be

Figure 9. Organisation of the single family office

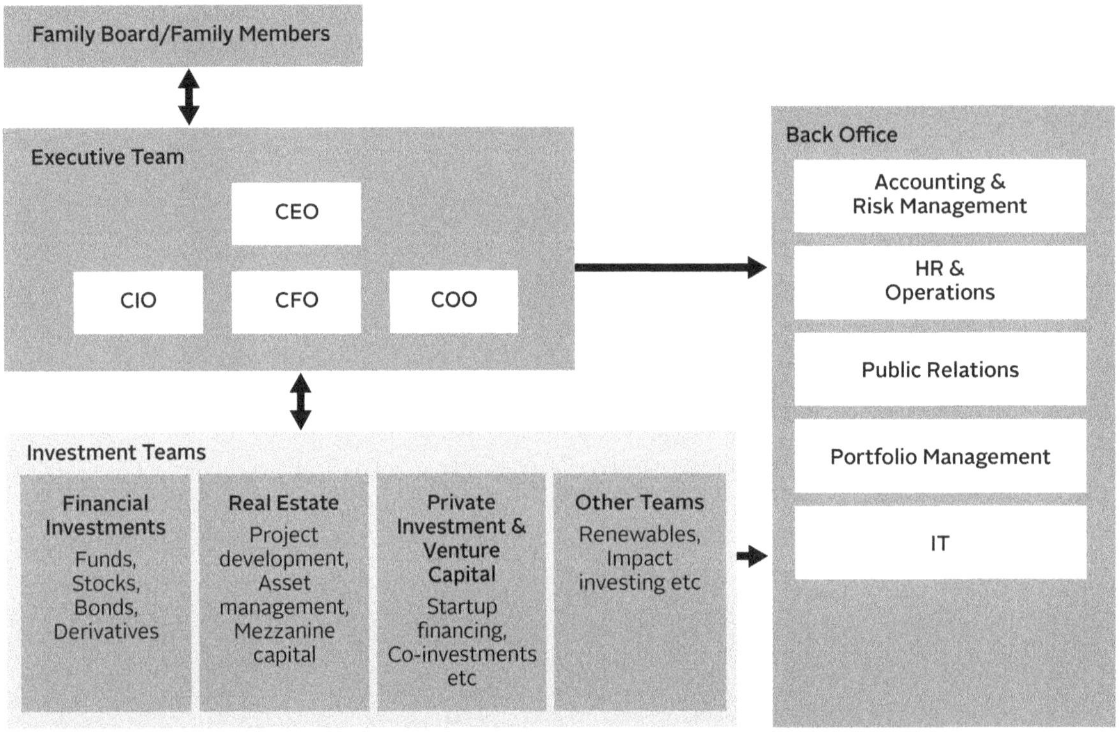

Source: familyofficehub.io – the knowledge platform for and about family offices

complicated – it could be as straightforward as a documented set of processes that support the management and ownership of your family's capital.

The key things to consider are:

- the kind of infrastructure that will best meet the family's needs; and
- how the structure of the family office will operate in practice.

Start with these questions:

- What will a normal day in the life of the office look like? Who will be doing what for whom? As far as possible, examine how simple matters will be delivered. How are tasks currently performed (assuming the functions of the family office are being transferred from the family business)? How will bank accounts operate? The list is long but working through these issues will pay dividends and ensure that you put the office infrastructure on a sound footing before investing the family's capital.
- What systems will the family office use, and how will internal systems interact with external provision? Working with your team, identify a list of possible areas to be handled by external

service providers. Include data, investment platforms, investment managers, brokers, accountants and anyone that your initial review shows will interact with the office.

- What do you want to know? How will you get a handle on what the family office is doing on behalf of you and your family?
- What is the purpose of the office? Remember that the overriding consideration is that the office must operate for the principals.

XIII. Governance

The governance of an SFO is often overlooked, when it is actually quite important. The family office needs to be treated with respect and to operate in a businesslike fashion, not simply reacting to the changing demands of family members. Without a professional approach the family office will find it difficult to attract and retain the staff essential to its success, and will risk confusion in respect of family members and their holdings.

The three key principles to keep in mind are:

- transparency;
- accountability; and
- participation.

Without transparency no one is sure about what is going on, and suspicions grow about whether some are treated more favourably than others.

Accountability means that when someone has agreed to take care of some matter, they will actually do so and will report their progress by way of an agreed mechanism. It is very easy for family members, or family office management, to agree to take care of something and then to do nothing. This perpetuates a culture where members no longer trust each other.

The third key principle is to encourage participation. We know of one family office that had been run by the eldest son, a benevolent dictator. When the family hired a consultant to help their family office get better organised and more efficient, one of the new proposals was to encourage hearing the views of all family members. As the eldest son told his peers:

> *I was very happy with the way I ran everything – then my siblings were encouraged to speak up and I learned that they had good ideas and different points of view. Now we have group discussions and I am happier – and our decisions are better.*

With the three principles in mind, a family office bears comparison to a company required to have formal quarterly meetings. The family members are like the shareholders of the company, and they – or a designated small group of them – will choose the head of the family office, just as shareholders choose a CEO.

1. Board of directors

We strongly recommend that from the beginning the family office has a board of directors. The quarterly board meetings are great motivators for the family office to report on the status of various projects, and to keep an official communication process open. The attendant transparency and accountability are valuable earmarks of success.

2. Committees

In the spirit of inclusion and participation, which we tend to favour in all family projects, we recommend that the board form a number of committees.

Committees are an excellent place to begin involving the next generation. We have seen a number of previously uninterested younger family members begin to take a serious interest when they are appointed to committee positions.

Committees might be constituted to:

- oversee the family trusts;
- monitor the investment performance; or
- ensure compliance with data privacy and social media guidelines.

Figure 10. Committees in context

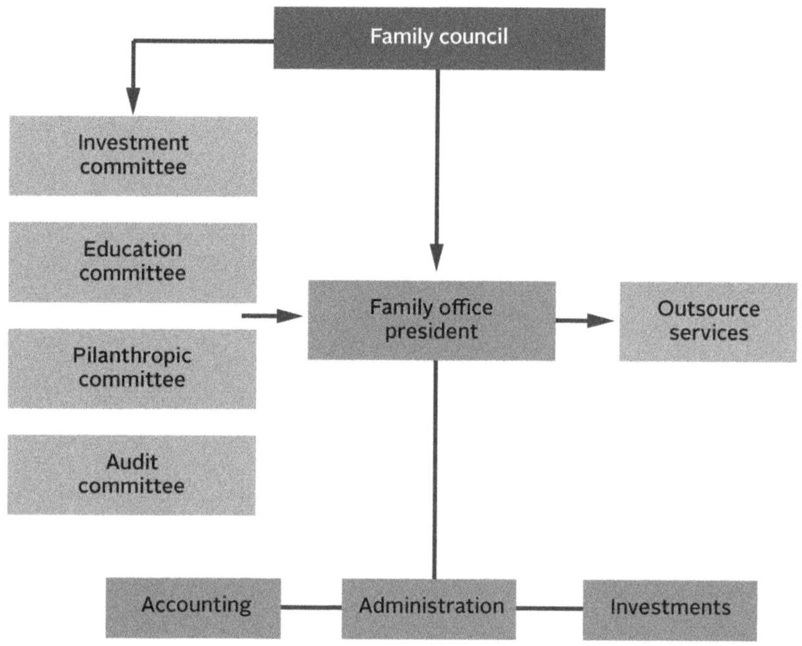

3. Family council

A family council, as the name implies, is a forum for family members to discuss matters that affect the 'family system' and how it impacts the family's wealth. It has no regulatory purpose nor, usually, any legal standing but it can be very important in ensuring that the family office remains fit for purpose.

As the family expands, the expectations placed upon the family office will change, and you may need to think about a family council, though it's possible you already have one established as part of the operation and governance of your family business.

The council may play a role in coordinating the work of committees designed to support the family office in delivering its purpose. In the office model illustrated, the family has developed several separate committees on which skilled and engaged family members serve. They include investment, education, philanthropic and audit committees.

4. Reporting to the family

The family office must always understand that it is serving the family. Frequent reports help prevent misunderstandings.

"From the outset, we suggest that you make tentative plans as to the potential lifespan of the family office. Do you intend to have it serve only the current family members or to continue for future generations?"

XIV. The life cycle of a family office

From the outset, we suggest that you make tentative plans as to the potential lifespan of the family office. Do you intend to have it serve only the current family members or to continue for future generations?

In the United States many of the family offices that were created by previous generations are now being scrutinised by current family members. The senior founding generation used to fund the office and no one had to worry about the costs. Those days come to an end sooner or later.

There are a number of ways in which the family can approach the future:

- They can continue in the same manner as before.
- They can open the doors of the family office to other families, with the hope of reducing the overhead. This is quite prevalent in the United States.
- They can dismantle the family office.
- They can partner with a larger office that will provide the administrative services, freeing a small group of the family office executives to interface with family members.

Leslie Voth quotes the CEO of one multi-generational family office that began as an SFO, who describes the natural stages:

> *Members of the next generation may ask whether there is a reason for the family office to stay intact. They may question whether they need the same services as their parents or grandparents, whether they want to continue paying the fees, whether they want more (or less) income than their predecessors, or whether they want to give the wealth away.*
>
> *The family members need to come together to develop a shared vision for the future. A positive decision to keep the services of the family office is more likely to be made if the office is able to demonstrate that it can successfully serve multiple generations.*
>
> *This means fostering transparency and open communication, choosing financial advisers who are right for the family, and making a commitment to educating and mentoring young family members as they mature into decision-makers.*[34]

If the time comes when the family decides to dismantle the office, that can be a complicated process. Voth describes one such case as follows:

> *One example is a family office that had been around for more than 50 years but was tied to an investment scandal that had significantly reduced the family's wealth. The scandal led family members to question the existence of the office, and since the office had been created by the patriarch and matriarch to meet their own needs, the children concluded that there was no point in funding it any longer.*
>
> *It took two years and a well-crafted transition plan for the family office to be completely unwound. There was a lot involved: the disposition of real estate, artwork, and furniture; scanning every record; building a website so the family could easily access everything; and reviewing the long-serving staff. One year was spent conducting the analysis and making tough decisions. The second year was the implementation of the plan.*[35]

Notes

1 The authors would like to thank Valerie Remoquillo-Jenni for her very helpful review of this report.
2 See G Baird, E Jamieson, M Kafena and S Rees, "United Kingdom" in *Family Offices: The STEP Handbook for Advisers*, 2nd edition, Globe Law and Business, 2019, p405.
3 Barbara R Hauser, "The Family Office: Insights into Their Development in the U.S., a Proposed Prototype, and Advice for Adaptation in Other Countries", *Journal of Wealth Management*, Fall 2001.
4 *Ibid*, p15.
5 H Hillerström, K McCracken and A Renkert-Thomas, "Family office governance" in *Family Offices – the STEP Handbook for Advisers*, Globe Law and Business, 2015, p167.
6 See *A Guide to Establishing a Family Office*, Citi Private Capital Group, 2018. Available at www.privatebank.citibank.com/ivc/docs/A-guide-to-establishing-a-family-office-Citi-Private-Bank.pdf.
7 See Armanino's website at www.armaninollp.com/services/private-wealth/family-office/.
8 For a detailed discussion of virtual family offices see Tom Handler, "Global virtual family offices" in Kirby Rosplock, *The Complete Family Office Handbook – A Guide for Affluent Families and the Advisors Who Serve Them*, Wiley, 2014, pp47–62.
9 The term 'financial family' gained currency in the context of the work of the Family Office Exchange, a membership body for family offices established in the US in 1989 by Sara Hamilton.
10 Russ Alan Prince, "How Much Money is Required to have a Single-Family Office?", Forbes website, October 2013. Available at: www.forbes.com/sites/russalanprince/2013/10/04/how-much-money-is-required-to-have-a-single-family-office/.
11 The Myer Family Investments vehicle was established for the benefit of the Myer Family and is based in Melbourne, Australia. See www.myerfamilyinvestments.com.au.
12 This is obviously the case for an SFO; in a multi-family office set-up, the office may serve more than one family.
13 For a discussion of this concept see Vic Preisser and Roy Williams, *Preparing Heirs: Five Steps to a Successful Transition of Family Wealth and Values*, Robert Read Publishers, 2010.
14 See the excellent analysis by Jan van Bueren and Thomas Ming, "Selecting the right family office jurisdiction" in Kirby Rosplock, *The Complete Family Office Handbook, supra*, pp35–46.
15 See Elizabeth Anderson, "Zero-based budgeting", *International Family Offices Journal*, September 2017.
16 See Racine Berkowitz, "Ten tips for the international movement of art", *The International Family Offices Journal*, December 2016.
17 For example, Hong Kong-based Qineticare. See www.qineticare.com.
18 Today in the United States, through the use of 'decanting', it is often possible to change older irrevocable trusts.
19 Jan van Bueren and Thomas Ming, "Family office jurisdictions: choosing the right one", *The International Family Offices Journal*, April 2018.
20 Agreus Group, "Family Office Structure – Organisational Considerations", July 2017. No longer available online.
21 Agreus Group, "Cultural Fit in Family Office Hiring", July 2019. Available at: www.agreusgroup.com/cultural-fit-in-family-office-hiring/.
22 MJ Rankin, "Recruitment and talent management strategies" in *Family Offices: The STEP Handbook for Advisers*, 2nd edition (Globe Law and Business, 2019), p75.
23 For a deeper discussion on this, see Catherine Grum and Edward Groves, "Rewards in the Family Office", in *The International Family Office Journal*, September 2017.
24 The real return is the income generated and capital growth of the portfolio after taking inflation into account .
25 The UBS/Campden Wealth *Global Family Office Report* offered an extensive analysis of costs as part of its 2019 survey. For a summary, see: www.campdenwealth.com/article/global-family-office-report-2019.
26 *A Guide to Establishing a Family Office,* Citibank, NA, 2018. Citibank, NA makes no representation as to the accuracy, adequacy, or completeness of the Citibank content and is not responsible for any errors or omissions or for the results obtained from its use.
27 See n 25 *supra.*
28 For a clear and very readable discussion on this approach, see Donald B Trone, William R Allbright and Philip R Taylor, *The Management of Investment Decisions*, McGraw-Hill, 1996.
29 Formed in 1989, the Family Office Exchange is an association providing analysis and support for its members, typically principals and executives of family offices. See: www.familyoffice.com/.
30 FOX, "Recasting the Central Role of the Family Office as Risk Manager", 2006. Summary of report available at: www.familyoffice.com/knowledge-center/recasting-central-role-family-office-risk-manager-new-imperative-family-risk.
31 Linda Bourn, "Risk and insurance management" in *Family Offices: The STEP Handbook for Advisers*, 2nd Edition, Globe Law and Business, 2019, p135.
32 Of course, it is important to protect the FO not just from cybercrime but from any crime.
33 See: www.qineticare.com.
34 Leslie Voth, "The lifecycle of the family office" in *Family Offices: The STEP Handbook for Advisers*, 2nd edition, Globe Law and Business, 2019, p233.
35 *Ibid.*

Additional resources

Organisations and conferences
Some of the most helpful information comes from joining family office associations and attending the many related conferences. You should ask families you know for advice as to organisations they find helpful. In the United States the first well-organised family office organisation was the Family Office Exchange (FOX) headquartered in Chicago, Illinois. There is a wealth of information on their website. They offer several categories of paid memberships. See www.familyoffice.com.

Also in the United States is the Family Office Association, based in New York, which is intended to consist solely of SFOs. They too hold conferences and there are a variety of papers on the website. They offer three categories of paid memberships. See www.familyofficeassociation.com.

Other more general conference organisations, and some financial institutions, offer the occasional conference focused on family offices. For example, the Hong Kong Institute of Science and Technology held well-attended day on family offices, with heavy attendance from mainland China. There are occasional family office conferences around the globe organised by Opal Financial Management, Camden Conferences, leading banks and others.

A number of the conferences are thinly disguised marketing events designed to find new clients, especially for investment services. Financial firms that sponsor these conferences often speak at them too, a 'pay to play' arrangement.

Books

The second edition of *The STEP Handbook for Advisers* (Globe Law and Business) was published earlier this year (2019). The book is divided into two parts: the first covers subjects relevant to most family offices, wherever located; the second has reports from a number of countries on how the family office market is developing in that jurisdiction.

In the United States, a second edition of *The Complete Family Office Handbook* by Kirby Rosplock (Bloomberg Press, 2014) is in preparation. Rosplock began by helping to manage her own family's wealth and developed an expertise in the family office field.

Family Legacy and Leadership: Preserving True Family Wealth in Challenging Times (Wiley Finance, 2010) is co-authored by Sara Hamilton, founder of FOX, and Mark Haynes Daniell.

Effective Family Office: Best Practices and Beyond (Family Office Publishing, 2017) is authored by Angelo Robles, founder of the Family Office Association.

See also the "Family Offices" chapter by Barbara Hauser and Melissa Langa, in *International Estate Planning: A Reference Guide* (Juris Publishing, 2018).

Periodicals

The International Family Offices Journal, a quarterly publication in its fourth year.

There are a few family office magazines that are largely devoted to either investment topics or the luxury retail market.

Selected articles

Barbara R Hauser, "The Family Office: Insights into Their Development in the U.S., a Proposed Prototype, and Advice for Adaptation in Other Countries", *Journal of Wealth Management*, Fall 2001.

Todd Ganos, "What is a family office?" Forbes online, 2013. Available at: www.forbes.com/sites/toddganos/2013/08/13/what-is-a-family-office/#333bfb7ba13f.

Barbara Hauser and Kirby Rosplock, "The Family Office Landscape: Today's Trends and Five Predictions for the Family Office of Tomorrow", *The Journal of Wealth Management*, Winter 2014.

About the authors

Barbara R Hauser
Independent family adviser
brhauser@gmail.com

Barbara Hauser has extensive experience advising families, family businesses and family offices, first as a private client lawyer and later with a focus on governance. She has helped families to develop their unique governance process, which may include a family constitution, a family council and a holding company board. She is a sought-after speaker and prolific writer, and is often referred to as a true thought leader in the family office field. Her books include *International Family Governance*, *International Estate Planning*, *Trusts in Prime Jurisdictions* (advisory editor), *Family Offices Handbook* (chapter entitled "Mommy, are we Rich?"); *Talking to Children about Family Money* (co-author); *Never Ask Where You Are*; *Saudi-Girl Barbara;* and *Selling Dog Food in Japan*.

Articles include "The Family Office: Insights into Their Development in the US, A Proposed Prototype and Advice for Adaptation in Other Countries", "Family Office Trends: Lessons from Dubai?" and "The Family Office Landscape: Today's Trends & Five Predictions for the Family Office of Tomorrow" (with Kirby Rosplock). Barbara is also the editor of Globe Law and Business's *International Family Offices Journal* and is listed in the Spears 500.

Keith Drewery
Director, Drewery Consulting
keith@dreweryconsulting.com

Keith Drewery has provided advice to private clients and their families for over thirty years. He began his career in London, emigrating to Sydney in 1994 and working for KPMG as a tax adviser. He then joined Perpetual Limited, working in national roles before becoming regional manager of its private client business.

In 2006, he opened the Sydney office of the Myer Family Office, at the time Australia's leading multi-family office, where he worked to develop the business in the Sydney marketplace. In 2012 he rejoined KPMG before starting his own consultancy practice.

Latterly his work has concentrated on consulting to wealth owners, family offices and professional services firms, with a focus on inter-generational wealth management services including succession and legacy development through philanthropy. Keith lives in Sydney and is married with three daughters.

About Globe Law and Business

Globe Law and Business was established in 2005, and from the very beginning we set out to create law books which are sufficiently high level to be of real use to the experienced professional, yet still accessible and easy to navigate. Most of our authors are drawn from Magic Circle and other top commercial firms, both in the UK and internationally.

Our titles are carefully produced, with the utmost attention paid to editorial, design and production processes. We hope this results in high-quality books which are easy to read, and a pleasure to own. All our new books are also available as ebooks, which are compatible with most desktop, laptop and tablet devices.

We have recently expanded our portfolio to include a new range of journals and Special Reports, available both digitally and in hard copy format, and produced to the same high standards as our books.

We'd very much like to hear from you with your thoughts and ideas for improving what we offer. Please do feel free to email me at sian@globelawandbusiness.com with your views.

Sian O'Neill
Managing director
Globe Law and Business